A Wetland Habitat

P9-CBR-979

Introducing Habitats

Molly Aloian and Bobbie Kalman

Crabtree Publishing Company

www.crabtreebooks.com

Created by Bobbie Kalman

Dedicated by Katherine Kantor: To Anna and Bryan Kivell
"Love to faults is always blind; Always is to joy inclined; Lawless, winged, and unconfined"

Editor-in-Chief
Bobbie Kalman

Writing team
Molly Aloian
Bobbie Kalman

Substantive editor
Kathryn Smithyman

Editors
Michael Hodge
Kelley MacAulay
Rebecca Sjonger

Design
Margaret Amy Salter
Samantha Crabtree (series logo)

Production coordinator
Heather Fitzpatrick

Photo research
Crystal Foxton

Special thanks to
Jack Pickett and Karen Van Atte

Illustrations
Barbara Bedell: page 32 (top)
Katherine Kantor: pages 5, 14-15, 23, 32 (bottom)
Bonna Rouse: page 17
Margaret Amy Salter: pages 14 (left), 28

Photographs
© Maier, Robert/Animals Animals - Earth Scenes: page 20
BigStockPhoto.com: title page, pages 19 (top left), 27 (top), 32 (middle center)
© Dwight Kuhn: page 21
iStockphoto.com: pages 18 (top and bottom), 19 (bottom right), 26, 27 (bottom)
Photo Researchers, Inc.: Suzanne L. and Joseph T. Collins: page 29;
      Michael P. Gadomski: page 13; Anthony Mercieca: page 30
robertmccaw.com: pages 9, 12, 16, 28, 31
Visuals Unlimited: John Sohlden: page 8
Other images by Adobe Image Library, Brand X Pictures, Corel, Digital Stock,
      Digital Vision, and Photodisc

Library and Archives Canada Cataloguing in Publication

Aloian, Molly
    A wetland habitat / Molly Aloian & Bobbie Kalman.
(Introducing habitats)
Includes index.
ISBN-13: 978-0-7787-2955-6 (bound)
ISBN-10: 0-7787-2955-9 (bound)
ISBN-13: 978-0-7787-2983-9 (pbk.)
ISBN-10: 0-7787-2983-4 (pbk.)
    1. Wetland ecology--Juvenile literature. I. Kalman,
Bobbie, date. II. Title. III. Series.

QH541.5.M3A46 2006   j577.68   C2006-904083-4

Library of Congress Cataloging-in-Publication Data

Aloian, Molly.
    A wetland habitat / Molly Aloian & Bobbie Kalman.
    p. cm. -- (Introducing habitats)
Includes index.
ISBN-13: 978-0-7787-2955-6 (rlb)
ISBN-10: 0-7787-2955-9 (rlb)
ISBN-13: 978-0-7787-2983-9 (pb)
ISBN-10: 0-7787-2983-4 (pb)
    1. Wetland ecology--Juvenile literature.   I. Kalman, Bobbie. II. Title.
QH541.5.M3A58 2006
577.68--dc22

2006018790

Crabtree Publishing Company

www.crabtreebooks.com   1-800-387-7650

Copyright © **2007 CRABTREE PUBLISHING COMPANY.** All rights reserved. No part of this publication may be reproduced, stored in a retrieval system or be transmitted in any form or by any means, electronic, mechanical, photocopying, recording, or otherwise, without the prior written permission of Crabtree Publishing Company. In Canada: We acknowledge the financial support of the Government of Canada through the Book Publishing Industry Development Program (BPIDP) for our publishing activities.

Printed in the USA/122009/CG20090903

Published in Canada
Crabtree Publishing
616 Welland Ave.
St. Catharines, ON
L2M 5V6

Published in the United States
Crabtree Publishing
PMB 59051
350 Fifth Avenue, 59th Floor
New York, New York 10118

Published in the United Kingdom
Crabtree Publishing
Maritime House
Basin Road North, Hove
BN41 1WR

Published in Australia
Crabtree Publishing
386 Mt. Alexander Rd.
Ascot Vale (Melbourne)
VIC 3032

Contents

What is a habitat?

A **habitat** is a place in nature. Plants live in habitats. Animals live in habitats, too. Some animals make homes in habitats.

Living and non-living things

There are **living things** in habitats. Plants and animals are living things. There are also **non-living things** in habitats. Rocks, water, and dirt are non-living things.

Everything they need

Plants and animals need certain things to stay alive. They need air, water, and food. Animals find everything they need in their habitats. This kingfisher found an insect to eat in its habitat.

Staying alive

This capybara lives in a habitat.
It finds everything it needs to stay
alive in its habitat. The capybara
needs water in its habitat. It
swims in the water.

What is a wetland?

A **wetland** is a habitat. A wetland is land that is covered with water. Some wetlands are covered with water all year. Other wetlands are covered with water only part of the year.

Wetlands called marshes

This book is about **marshes**.
Marshes are a kind of wetland.
Many plants and animals live
in marshes. This snapping
turtle lives in a marsh.

Marshes

Marshes are covered with water all year. They are along the edges of lakes, rivers, and ponds. These baby ducks find food in a marsh. They swim in the water.

A freshwater marsh

Some marshes have **salt water**. Salt water has a lot of salt in it. Other marshes have **fresh water**. Fresh water has only a little salt. This book is about freshwater marshes. This deer is drinking water from a freshwater marsh.

Marsh weather

Most marshes are in parts of the world that have four **seasons**. The seasons are spring, summer, autumn, and winter. The weather is different during each season. In spring, the weather is warm. In summer, the weather is hot.

Cold winters

The weather in a marsh becomes chilly during autumn. The weather gets cold in winter. In winter, there is snow and ice in a marsh. The water in this marsh is frozen.

Marsh plants

bur reed

cattails

Many kinds of
plants grow in
marshes. Bur reeds
and cattails grow
in water. They grow
along the edges of
marshes. The water
is shallow near the
edges of marshes.

14

Water plants

Some marsh plants grow in the middle of marshes. These water lilies are growing in the middle of a marsh. They have large green leaves. The leaves float on top of the water.

Plants make food

Living things need food to stay alive.
Plants make their own food. They
make food using sunlight, air, and
water. Making food from sunlight, air,
and water is called **photosynthesis**.

Parts for making food

A plant gets sunlight through its leaves. It also gets air through its leaves. A plant gets water through its roots. A plant uses sunlight, air, and water to make food.

Leaves take in air.

Leaves take in sunlight.

Roots take in water from the soil. The soil is at the bottom of marshes.

Marsh animals

Many animals live in marshes. The animals on these pages are marsh animals. Marsh animals have bodies that are suited to their marsh habitats.

A crayfish can breathe under water.

*A duck's feathers are **waterproof**.*
Waterproof feathers stay dry in water.

A newt is a good swimmer.
It moves its tail from side to side to swim.

A water strider can walk on the top of water.

A raccoon uses its paws to pick up food and put it into its mouth.

This heron uses its long beak to catch food to eat.

This snail finds plenty of plants to eat in a marsh.

Living in water

Some marsh animals live only in water. They find food in water. This fish lives in water. It has body parts called **fins**. It uses its fins to swim.

fins

Tadpoles

This animal is a **tadpole**. A tadpole is a baby frog. A tadpole lives in water. It is a good swimmer. It eats plants that are in the water.

On the edges

Many marsh animals spend time on the edges of marshes. They go into the water to swim. They also look for food in the water. This muskrat goes into the water to find food.

Food in the water

The water at the edge of a marsh is shallow. This spoonbill is standing in the shallow water. It grabs small fish from the water using its long beak.

Blending in

It is hard to see some marsh animals. This rabbit has brown fur. The reeds and grasses around the rabbit are also brown. The rabbit blends in with the reeds and grasses. Other animals may find it hard to see the rabbit in its marsh habitat.

Good to be green

This frog is green. The lily pads around the frog are also green. The frog blends in with the green lily pads. Other animals may have trouble seeing the green frog when it sits on a lily pad.

Finding food

There is plenty of food in marshes.
Some animals eat only plants.
Animals that eat plants are called
herbivores. Beavers are herbivores.
They eat bark and other plant parts.

Eating other animals

Other marsh animals are **carnivores**. Carnivores eat other animals. This alligator is a carnivore. It eats fish, turtles, and snakes.

Omnivores

Some marsh animals are **omnivores**. Omnivores eat both plants and animals. A skunk is an omnivore. It eats grass, leaves, insects, and fish.

Getting energy

All living things need **energy**. They need energy to grow and to move. Energy comes from the sun. Plants get energy from the sun. Animals cannot get energy from the sun. They get energy by eating other living things. A tadpole is a herbivore. It gets energy by eating plants in water.

sun

plants

tadpole

Eating for energy

Carnivores get energy
by eating other animals.
A northern water snake is
a carnivore. It gets energy
by eating tadpoles.

Making homes

Some marsh birds make homes called **nests**. In spring, these birds lay eggs in their nests. Baby birds hatch from the eggs. They are called **chicks**. The chicks live in the nests. These harrier chicks are safe in their nest.

An otter in the water

This otter made its home inside
a hole. The otter's home is called a
den. The den is at the side of a marsh.
The otter is coming out of its den.

Words to know and Index

animals
pages 4, 5, 6, 9, 18-19, 20, 21, 22, 24, 25, 26, 27, 28, 29

energy
pages 28-29

food
pages 6, 10, 16, 17, 19, 20, 22, 23, 26-27

habitats
pages 4, 5, 6, 7, 8, 18

marshes
pages 9, 10, 11, 12, 13, 14, 15, 18, 19, 20, 22, 23, 24, 26, 27, 30, 31

nests
page 30

Other index words

plants
pages 4, 5, 6, 9, 14-15, 16, 17, 19, 21, 26, 27, 28

water
pages 5, 6, 7, 8, 10, 11, 13, 14, 15, 16, 17, 18, 19, 20, 21, 22, 23, 28, 29, 31